WEEKS 52 change your world

Allan Shepherd and Caroline Oakley

© CAT Publications 2004
The Centre for Alternative Technology Charity Ltd
Machynlleth, Powys, SY20 9AZ, UK
Tel. 01654 705980 Fax. 01654 702782
email: pubs@cat.org.uk web: www.cat.org.uk www.ecobooks.co.uk
Registered Charity No. 265239

ISBN 1 90217 518 2
1 2 3 4 5 6 7 8 9 10

Design: Graham Preston & Paul Bullen

Mail Order copies from: Buy Green By Mail, Tel. 01654 705959
The details are provided in good faith and believed to be correct at the time of
writing, however no responsibility is taken for any errors. Our publications are
updated regularly; please let us know of any amendments or additions which you
think may be useful for future editions.

Printed in Great Britain by Cambrian Printers (01970 627111)
on paper obtained from sustainable sources.

Acknowledgements

The authors and CAT would like to thank Aveda (whose decision to make CAT an Earth Month partner prompted the first discussions) for being the catalyst that made this book happen. Also, Suzanne Galant, Hele Oakley, Graham Preston and Paul Bullen for feedback, proofing and design. We'd also like to thank all those environmentalists, including our colleagues at CAT, who post their information on the web for the edification of all – we hope we have taken your work and made it accessible to those who otherwise might not go looking...

Introduction

52 Weeks is a primer for the planet – pick it up and sort out your priorities...

Time is a precious commodity – one that we never seem to have quite enough of (just like money!). But it isn't just short for us individually...too many people are living the kind of lives that mean time is running out for the world, unless we change our ways and soon – current estimates from climate scientists put it at just 50 years. *52 Weeks to Change Your World* is a little book of good things for you and for the earth – weekly suggestions for changes big and small, simple and tricky, that you can make to improve the earth's balance of payments. Little changes made by lots of people can add up to a big improvement in environmental conditions, so start small in week one and work up to something more radical if you can. Not everyone can become the leader of a G8 nation, but we can all make a difference.

Use good design to beat global warming...

Change your light bulbs. Most of us are using light bulbs designed at the start of the 20th century. This is a crime against progress and a waste of energy. Most of the electrical energy pumping into an ordinary light bulb turns into heat – ever tried to change a light bulb when it's on? We shouldn't be using light bulbs to heat our rooms, they're just not designed to do the job. Low energy light bulbs turn the energy into light and not heat.

This is your first step towards tackling the biggest man-made environmental problem the world has ever known – global warming. By changing your light bulbs you cut your emissions of the greenhouse gas carbon dioxide (CO_2), which causes global warming. Carbon dioxide occurs naturally in the earth's atmosphere. It is called a greenhouse gas because it keeps the earth warm by trapping heat from the sun in the atmosphere – in much the same way as glass traps heat in a greenhouse. Without it life as we know it would be impossible. Unfortunately, we have put so much carbon dioxide into the atmosphere that too much heat from the sun is being trapped on earth. The earth is getting hotter and no one is quite sure what this will mean for weather conditions. Most climate experts say life on earth will become more and more intolerable if we don't cut CO_2 emissions.

By changing our light bulbs we are deploying a primary weapon against global warming – good design.

And you'll save money! Each low energy light bulb saves £7 worth of electricity a year, and they last 12 times as long as prehistoric light bulbs – so fewer trips to the shops. In fact you don't even need to leave the house to get them. Get them from www.cat.org.uk/shop, 01654 705959; or, for a wider choice, www.bltdirect.co.uk.

Get out the garden bench...

This week is all about making eco-friendly consumer choices –
it's not just any old garden bench that will do!

How to make the right choice...

There's lots you can do as a consumer to help persuade the retail
industry that you won't stand for the exploitation of the natural
world. Illegal logging is a constant and ongoing threat to the
world's forests – in both hemispheres, in the East and West. The
best option is to look for the fsc – Forestry Stewardship Council –
logo: this WWF sponsored non-governmental organisation has been
set up as an eco-labelling authority for timber and timber products
sourced from sustainably managed forests. It guarantees a chain of
supply that should prevent products coming from illegal logging
(either in Indonesia, the Amazon or the ancient forests of Finland
and Russia). There are other eco-labels for wood, but they don't
guarantee the whole supply chain: illegal logging takes place not
just when timber is harvested, but when it is transported, bought or
sold in violation of national laws. The worst excesses often relate to

tropical hardwood – where you can, look for softwood products – and beware particularly of products like plywood, which are notorious for their illegal connections. A UK–Indonesia joint study of the industry from 1998 identified 40% of Indonesia's output as illegal, and more recent estimates suggest that a total 70% of timber in the country is illegal in one way or another*.

Where to find that eco-friendly bench...
Visit your local DIY store or garden centre and ask to be shown only benches with the fsc logo. If they don't stock one ask why, and then shop elsewhere. Or log on to www.fsc-uk.info and look for their products directory and stockist information.

*www.illegal-logging.info

Learn to breathe...

Anyone who practises yoga will know how important and neglected the process of breathing is. Despite the fact that we breathe in and out over 21,600 times a day we are barely aware of it. Unless, that is, we happen to be one of the 100 million people around the world suffering from asthma (a figure which is growing by 50% every decade), or the many millions more suffering from other respiratory disorders and lung diseases such as allergies, hay fever and emphysema.

Respiratory disorders and disease can be caused or exacerbated by microscopic particles found in pollutants, but there are lots of things that quite simply take your breath away: smoking; damp houses with poor ventilation; carpets; dust, allergens; mould; certain paints; emotional distress; some types of medication.

People suffering from stress will also become more aware of breathing problems. Stress forces rapid, shallow breaths, reducing oxygen intake and inducing lethargy. Some people try to reduce stress levels by smoking, drinking or just plain slobbing out. Because of this, long-term stress is worse for the heart than putting on 40lbs.

So, the first task of the 'breathe easy' challenge is to find out about breathing, and do something pleasant to reduce your own stress levels. A very good start is www.yogaatwork.co.uk. It offers work-based yoga consultancies for companies, as well as a number of other services, but the website also contains some useful information about breathing and some basic breathing exercises to get you started. If you haven't already begun looking into alternative therapies, spa treatments and meditation, now is the time. Also take a look at your own home and if you have breathing problems see if there might be an obvious cause. If you want advice about asthma contact the British Lung Foundation which runs the Breathe Easy Club (www.britishlungfoundation.org).

WEEK 4

Set up your own sustainable water supply...

This week it's time to open up the shed and put your working gloves on. Fitting a rainwater butt is relatively cheap and easy – one of those small things that if replicated worldwide would ease the increasing pressure on the planet's over-stretched number one natural resource: clean water.

Why it's important to recycle your rainwater...

- there's a global shortage of drinking quality water – sprinkling or hosepiping it onto the garden isn't necessary
- climate change will lead to more precipitation (that's rain, snow and hail to the uninitiated), but also to more evaporation
- the extra wet stuff won't be falling where it's most needed
- climate change will mean alternate floods and droughts, so water storage in times of plenty will be essential
- thanks to the thermal expansion of the oceans, higher sea levels will impact on coastal water supplies, pushing salt water further inland along rivers, deltas and aquifers (underground streams)
- water security: even the UK's water is now largely owned by

foreign corporations; in the US they're piping it from coast to coast to meet Californian demand

Where do I get the goods?
- Any decent high street ironmonger, garden centre or DIY store will have the wherewithal for you to fit an 'in-line' water butt to your guttering and drainpipes. If you can, try and find a non-PVC plastic butt with a lid (to prevent contamination). And don't forget to fit an overflow diverter back into the pipe if yours is a simple water butt: telephone Rain Drain Ltd for a Rain-Sava: 01924 468564
- If saving your rainwater encourages you to do more, get hold of a copy of CAT's Water Conservation tipsheet from www.ecobooks.co.uk or by calling 01654 705959

WEEK
4

Be a patron of the arts...

Forget Scrap Heap Challenge, if you really want to see someone do something creative with rubbish take a look at David Owen's website www.metalsculpture.f9.co.uk. Based in North Wales, David uses plentiful local waste materials (old caravans, discarded boilers, drift wood), and turns them into functional art pieces such as gates, chairs, and bird tables. He is just one member of a thriving community of artisans turning rubbish into art, who are in turn the tip of an iceberg of industrious and creative types making good use of the things everyday people leave behind. If you want to get really excited about 'wombling' industries get hold of a copy of *The Eco-Design Handbook* by Alastair Fuad-Luke – as far as we're concerned one of the most inspiring books on the environment.

Your task this week is quite simple. To support the recycling industry go out, or stay in if you've got the Internet, and buy at least one item that has been made out of 100% recycled materials. We don't care whether it's as simple as a pen made out of vending cups (www.remarkable.co.uk) or as complicated as Julienne Dolphin

Wilding's 100-piece armchair made out of salvaged yew (www.julienne.demon.co.uk). You could get hold of an interesting garden feature from www.salvo.co.uk or some tailored office equipment from www.reactivated.co.uk. Check out the product directory at www.rethinkrubbish.com. Items for sale include fashion accessories, clothes, kids' toys and stuff for the home and garden.

Get in some guilt free treats for Friday night...

Not so much something to do as a little pat on the back for all your other environmentally friendly efforts: pop out and pick up a bar, or box, of organic Fair Trade choc's.

How it helps combat environmental damage...

Organic farming relies much more on traditional methods than modern day industrial agriculture, which looks to pesticide and fertiliser dependent mono-crops for its profits. The small-scale farmers in Belize, whose Mayan ancestors first domesticated the cacao tree, cannot compete with big business and need to find other ways to make their staple crop economic to grow. Securing long-term contracts for organically grown cocoa beans means environmental, health and financial benefits (organic crops attract premium prices; Fair Trade labelling guarantees a fair rather than market engineered price). Growing several varieties of cacao tree alongside other food, fibre and medicinal plant species creates a biodiverse landscape, which lessens the dangers to susceptible crops from pest and disease attack. This in turn reduces or removes the need for pesticides that are potentially damaging to human health and indigenous flora and fauna.

What to do and how to do it...
Walk out the door, into your nearest corner shop or supermarket and look for organic and Fair Trade labels in the confectionary aisle. Or log on to: www.greenandblacks.co.uk or www.fairtrade.org.uk for information on stockists.

Plant a plant...

Everyone knows that trees absorb carbon dioxide and give us oxygen in return – it is not without reason that the Amazonian rainforests are called the lungs of the planet – but people sometimes forget that every other plant on the planet is doing the same. This week's breathe easy challenge is to increase plant life on the planet. Sounds a bit daunting when you read it like that, but we're not talking about Eden Projects here. You could just dig up a concrete patio and replace it with some easy to maintain perennial border plants. A few house plants around the place can improve air quality. BC Wolverton's book *Eco-friendly Houseplants* starts off by describing what NASA has found out about indoor pollution before going on to describe 50 plants that can combat it.

Look out for any of the following:
- Golden Pothos – to combat carbon monoxide
- Spiky Cactus (*Cereus peruvianus*) – to combat radiation
- Spider plants and Boston ferns – to combat formaldehyde
- Chysanthemums and English ivy – to combat benzene
- Peace lilies – to combat trichlorethylene

If you want to be a bit more adventurous and you haven't got a garden, you could start thinking about the structure of your house as a garden. Some of the most exciting green home projects have incorporated green roofs. These can be made out of turf dotted with daffodils or low maintenance options such as sedum. Not only do green roofs improve air quality by absorbing airborne particles but they can also help to control localised flooding by absorbing rainwater and insulating the house. CAT has a Turf Roof tipsheet – see www.ecobooks.co.uk
Also try www.erisco-bauder.co.uk for more information.

And if you don't have the space or time to think about growing your own plants then there's a range of charities who'll do it for you, of which www.plantlife.org.uk, www.treesforlife.org.uk, www.woodland-trust.org.uk are just three.

Trash toxic waste...

This week your task is quite straightforward, just a little matter of logging-on or licking a stamp. If you haven't done it already, put your money where your mouth is and join a campaign group who'll use your cash, and/or physical support, to stop toxic trash being dumped on your doorstep.

An example of what you might help put a stop to...

Towards the end of 2003, research and legal action by Friends of the Earth proved that the company Able UK had no legal right to fulfil its contract with the US Government to break up and dispose of a number of warships containing toxic chemicals called PCBs. It is illegal for this chemical waste to be dumped by the US Government. in the USA(!), but apparently it is legal for the US Government. to dump their toxic waste in the UK, provided that the requisite licences are in place (how logical is that?). However, thanks to FoE lawyers, the Seaton Meadows landfill in Hartlepool is currently safe from the 'ghost ships', as the press dubbed them. Not only do Able UK not have the appropriate licences in place, they've had licences suspended as recently as February 2001 for contraventions of Environment Agency landfill conditions for licences relating to leachate management and monitoring systems. (Leachate is the liquid that forms as water runs through landfilled waste.)

Thanks to campaigners like you, nearby Seaton Dunes and Seaton Common, both specially protected conservation areas, are protected from the 'ghost ships'' toxic leachate. For the moment, at least...

What to do and how to do it...

Contact Friends of the Earth for membership information and join up

- by mail: 26-28 Underwood Street, London N1 7JQ
- by telephone: 020 7490 1555
- online: www.foe.org.uk

For more info on PCBs check out the FoE factsheet online.

Recycle, recycle, recycle...

If a problem is a solution waiting to happen, rubbish in the UK is a problem. Every year we up our production of rubbish by almost one million tonnes, with most of the annual total of 26 million tonnes going straight to landfill. And whilst our European neighbours are nudging their recycling rates up to 50%, at 11% we've only just got into double figures. This week it's time to nudge up your own recycling rate. Whatever you're doing at the moment, the chances are there's always room to improve. Your challenge is to include at least one new item in your recycling programme – be it one of the regulars such as paper, card or bottles (phone your local council for recycling information), or something slightly more exotic such as books (info@prismproject), batteries (www.rebat.com) or bicycles (www.re-cycle.org).

Ink cartridges are one of the easiest things to recycle and yet hardly anyone does. Two million are thrown away every year. ActionAid operates a very successful cartridge recycling business and the profits support charitable projects in the developing world. Visit www.nru.org.uk for details. Office workers who send off their printer cartridges can put a certificate of thanks up on the wall to encourage others to do the same. Rather than turn your mobile phone into a statistic (one of the 15 million thrown out every year), send it to Action Aid (www.actionaid.org) or Oxfam (www.oxfam.org.uk) instead of the dustbin.

Find out what it's like to live on a Pacific island...

As the weeks go by you will be able to reduce your share of carbon emissions to the point where your life on this planet is sustainable. Whilst most of these measures will not inconvenience you in the slightest, and may well improve your life, some of them will result in...here goes...sacrifice.

Sacrifice is one of those words environmentalists try to steer clear of because it conjures up old-fashioned images of bearded men in hair shirts, spinning yarn by candlelight. But, until technology catches up with global warming, the chances are that we will all have to give up something. But keep the faith. By giving up something you may well be giving someone else life.

In preparation for this moment of pure altruism, the task in week ten is to find out what it's like to be President Gayoom of the Maldives – he is losing one third of his country's beaches to rising water levels caused by global warming. Or imagine what it's like for the fishermen of Tebua Tarawa and Abanuear (which, ironically, means the beach that is long lasting) who have now lost these two islands to the sea; or even the five million people who are currently at danger of severe flooding in the UK. Start off with www.uk.yahoo.com, type in global warming+flooding+islands and see what comes up. Find out how flooding damages housing, disrupts and destroys lives, spreads disease and ruins agricultural land.

Detergent free dirty linen...

You can wash your poshest frocks or grubbiest football kit without worrying about the planetary consequences, if you remember to think phosphate first.

Alternatives to the washday blues...

Phosphate is another of those terribly useful chemicals (good for root growth where it occurs naturally in the soil beneath your sunflowers) that, used in the wrong place for the wrong job, can also exert unforeseen stress on natural resources. Each time you put powder or liquid into your washer it'll end up surging through the sewers and eventually discharging into a watercourse. Once in the water it'll reduce the oxygen available to fish and other water creatures and change the habitat for plants and algae (just like the nitrates in agricultural run-off). But there are alternatives – like the eco-ball, which, when thrown in with the washing, does the job of the phosphate – preventing the dirt settling back onto the fibres of your clothes. Eco-balls produce ionized oxygen that allows water molecules to penetrate deep into clothing fibres to lift dirt away.

There are no harsh chemicals, so less pollution. And rinse cycles can be shortened, saving water and electricity. If you can't get hold of eco-balls or similar devices, there are detergents available with alternatives to phosphate in them that are kinder to the environment than conventional powders.

So where do I get the alternatives from?
- CAT Mail Order: tel. 01654 705959
- Check out an online eco-retailer: www.cat.org.uk/shop; www.ecozone.co.uk; www.21stcenturyhealth.co.uk

It's holiday time – take a break with a difference...

There's a lot you can do, from combining a beach holiday with habitat conservation to taking a weekend break that keeps you fit and polishes up your environmental halo. After all, if you must fly out to the sun you might as well repair some of the damage caused by your jumbo jet's exhaust.

Get in touch with your holiday hero...

There are heaps of opportunities for holidaying nationally and internationally. You can take a trip to Africa and work on coastal management and marine biodiversity in The Gambia – live and work alongside local people and visit local markets and discos (catch a kora band concert if you can, and look out for the accompanying male dance troupe – Pan's People eat your heart out!). In New Zealand there are chances to work on re-establishing wetland valleys and live in a traditional Maori Marae. Nearer to home you could help sustain a long-term programme of canal bed management by restoring open water areas and turning a disused canal in Nottinghamshire into a safe haven for water voles and dragonflies. Or you could help out a new European neighbour by working on flood plain management alongside the River Danube in Slovakia. The choice is yours…and don't forget, every little bit of reclamation work helps repair some of the damage done by water pollution and misuse.

Here's how to book…
• BTCV Conservation Holidays: tel. 01302 572244; www.btcv.org
…and if you don't fancy these just nip down to the library, or up to the spare room, log on to a search engine and type in 'conservation holidays'.

Get Moving on GM...

Time to lobby the Prime Minister; get him and his civil servants thinking about the genetic modification of food plants, and what it means for the species that have evolved over millions of years to make the most of their natural habitat – plants, animals and micro-creatures alike.

Why are GM crops a problem?

One of the biggest threats to our native plant life is the mono-cropping beloved of modern agriculture. Densely planted mono-crops are dependent on the large-scale use of fertilizers and pesticides to avoid the danger of crop loss due to infestation or disease. In their turn, the pesticides impact on pollinating insects, the bird population and soil creatures. Not only that, but the destruction of hedgerows, for the creation of fields in which industrial scale machines can function effectively, cuts down on biodiversity even further. The next step is genetically modified crops designed to work even more closely with pesticides and fertilizers. These impact yet further on the range of plants able to grow in and around prairie-sized fields of grain, beet or potatoes. They may even prove to have the ability to cross-breed with organic crops, meaning that non-GM crops will no longer be an option – whether GM proves a problem or not.

So what can I do about it?

- Write to the PM at the House of Commons, and send a copy to the head of DEFRA
- Lobby for subsidies and tax incentives for organic farming, or for 'set aside' to be used for native meadow plants or coppice planting
- Ask your local councillors to make your community GM free, like Totnes
- Don't buy GM food and tell your shopkeeper why; ask your local supermarket to stop selling meat reared on GM feed
- If you're feeling a bit radical, take the Green Gloves pledge! www.greengloves.org

Make a packet from a racket...

Invent another use for at least one thing in your house that you don't want any more. If you're feeling adventurous you could follow the example of Brian May: Queen's guitarist and one time Buck House troubador made his world famous Red Special (guitar) with the help of his dad when he was knee-high to a Fender® Stratocaster. They made the guitar from unusual pieces of (scrap) wood, such as oak and various old electrical parts found lying around the house. If your carpentry and electrical skills don't quite stretch that far you could apply yourself to a less ambitious project; like a drumstick.

If you're a gardener with a slug problem you can kill two birds with one stone and replace your chemical slug pellets with a wide range of home-made solutions: beer traps made out of old yoghurt pots; protective cloches for seedlings from plastic bottles; upturned grapefruit skins attract slugs; old copper rings or wire give them a mild electric shock; and so on (see CAT's *Little Book of Slugs* for more).

Arty types could check out their local night school for a course on home dyeing techniques for old clothes. We found one on the Internet that showed participants how to dye fabrics using things like onion skins, and turn the results into scarfs, bandanas or cards. If you want some inspiration try any one of the following books: *Eco Deco – chic, ecological design using recycled materials* by Stewart and Sally Walton, *The Resourceful Renovator – a gallery of ideas for re-using building materials* by Jenifer Corson, and *The Fine Art of The Tin Can* by Bobby Hanson (all available from CAT: 01654 705959; cat.org.uk/shop).

A walk in the woods...

Take a walk with your closest friends and help maintain the UK's native woodland habitat. Once heavily forested, the UK now has one of the lowest figures for woodland acreage in Europe. Our remaining ancient woodland covers less than 2% of the country. Catch it while you can...

What can I do to ensure this habitat isn't lost?

You can help keep woods on the map by joining the Woodland Trust.

Woods are crucial to sustaining life on earth. They take in carbon dioxide and return oxygen to the atmosphere. Many species of native flora and fauna depend on woodland for their survival. The Woodland Trust exists to protect, restore and enhance forests and woods in the UK. And it doesn't just look out for ancient forests: creating new woodland is a major part of its work. The UK Biodiversity Action Plan identifies broadleaved woodland as supporting almost twice as many species of conservation concern as any other habitat, i.e. more than twice as many as chalk grassland and almost three times as many as lowland heathland*.

There are Woodland Trust woods all over the UK and there's a directory specifying those that have marked walks and facilities such as picnic areas. There's sure to be one nearby that'll give you an insight into what we stand to lose if our native wildlife is harried out of existence. Perhaps you'll be inspired to buy your own patch of woodland – alone or in a group – conservation is easy when you know how.

Useful contacts
- Woodland Trust: The Woodland Trust, Autumn Park, Grantham, Lincolnshire, NG31 6LL; 01476 581135; www.woodland-trust.org.uk
- For small woodlands for sale visit www.woodlands.co.uk, or write to Woodland Investment Management, 35 Giant Arches Road, London SE24 9HP

*Woodland Trust website

Get turned on to green electricity...

If you completed week ten's task you will now have a good idea as to how global warming is changing people's lives in thousands of places around the world. Now you can find out how to change your home life to stop it happening. People living in the developed world create several times more carbon dioxide per person than those in developing countries. And yet it would be quite easy for most of us to dramatically reduce this imbalance by switching to clean technologies that cost little or no more than dirty ones.

Home energy use accounts for 25% of CO_2 emissions in the UK. Although a complete energy audit of your house is the most effective way to cut CO_2 emissions in the home, and save you money, this may take some organising. So for simplicity's sake, your next anti-global warming task is to buy green electricity. This is easy to do, but as there are several schemes to choose from you may have to spend a bit of time weighing up the pros and cons of each one. Most suppliers charge no more for green electricity and some give you extra incentives for doing so. For example Juice

(npower), will donate £10 to CAT for every CAT member that signs up. www.greenelectricity.org gives impartial information on all green tariffs,
as does Friends of the Earth (tel. 020 7490 1555)
and the Energy Saving Trust (tel.0800 512 012).

Be real about fires...

Rustic romantics long for the cosy glow of a solid fuel fire, but solid fuels are (unromantically) bad for the local environment. Damp unseasoned (i.e. freshly cut) wood in particular is a very bad burner, releasing much higher levels of fine particulates (PM10) than dry wood. This can cause breathing difficulties and lower oxygen levels in a room making the occupants feel drowsy. It is very difficult to get hold of dry seasoned wood, and although smokeless coal fuels are worse for global warming than wood, they are better for local pollution (an interesting dilemma).

So, what to do?
Get hold of a paper log maker and turn your newspapers into a burnable log, or if you prefer a less hands-on approach to the good life a greener alternative is to invest in a more efficient wood stove or one that burns wood chip pellets. The pellets are made from waste wood, sawdust and shavings. Most work on a feeder system, so you only have to tend to them every couple of days. You can also control the heat using a small electric fan, thus combining a real flame with full controllability and efficiency.

Visit www.ecodyfi.org.uk for comparisons on wood burning stoves, community wood stoves and pellet burners.

Even if you have your own wood supply from garden trimmings you would be better off with a pellet burner. You should also avoid garden bonfires. Damp garden materials burnt on an open fire will release carbon monoxide, dioxins and particulates. Instead of burning it, hire a small wood chipper (see Yellow Pages), turn it into compost, and use it as a nice mulch to suppress weeds on your flowerbed.

Launder your cash and clean up your conscience...

Provided you aren't a millionaire or thousands in debt, this week's change should be reasonably easy to make, though it requires a bit of research and an element of personal choice.

What's money got to do with my environment?

Ethical finance is all about directing your savings towards companies whose activities have a positive, rather than negative, impact on society or the environment. It isn't difficult to buy shares in an ecologically sound company via the stockmarket, once you've identified it, but this isn't all you can do... Ordinary banking services, mortgages and pensions can be bought ethically too. A number of finance companies and independent financial advisors now exist to help you invest in savings and other schemes based on a portfolio of environmental likes and dislikes. For example, the Ecology Building Society's mortgages are designed specifically for clients buying energy efficient houses or wanting to build from sustainable or recycled materials.

The Co-operative Bank has had an ethical policy since 1992 and 97% of its two million customers support its position. Triodos Bank lends 'exclusively to organisations that are pursuing positive social, environmental and cultural goals' (James Niven, Triodos). So, check out the options and let your money talk.

Where do I go for independent advice?
Speak to an FSA approved independent financial advisor – you'll find them in the phone book or online: they should give impartial advice.
Or check online for ethical specialists including Ethical Investors Group, www.ethicalinvestors.co.uk; tel. 01242 539848.

Celebrate fresh air in Wales...

The Wales Tourist Board recently employed the Mayor of London's Town Crier to promote National Fresh Air Day to deck chair users in The Royal Parks of St James and Green Park. This week's challenge is to come and visit the Dyfi Valley in Powys, Wales, the home of The Centre for Alternative Technology (CAT), and remember what fresh air is really like. OK it's a bit of an advertorial this week, but we wouldn't recommend it if it wasn't a really good way to spend a few days.

Not only will you clear your chest of whatever carbon based particulates you've been inhaling recently, you'll see what it's like to live with renewable energy, find out how to compost rather than burn your garden rubbish, and to be able to buy green outdoor fuels, log makers, non-toxic paints (see the next breathe easy challenge) and books about yoga, and house plants. If you explore the local area you'll be able to climb a mountain, swim in the sea (well, at least get your knees wet) and enjoy some of the local alternative therapies on offer in the area.

If you're a teacher, we have residential and day visit facilities for national curriculum focused activities. If you're in the mood for some learning we have over 40 residential courses on offer, ranging from rustic furniture making and willow sculpture to building your own wind turbine. And after all that, if you can't get enough of CAT you can become a member and get our quarterly magazine. See www.cat.org.uk. But beware, some people come to the Dyfi Valley for a few days and stay for the rest of their lives!

Get reading, get genned up...

Join a book group and get others to read your choice of book –
make it one that will tickle their little grey cells: see if you can
convert a few sceptics!

Which books might stimulate the debate?
There's a wide range of choice, from modern classics to titles hot
off the press. Why not try *Silent Spring* by Rachel Carson or
Somewhere Under the Sun by John O'Neill, which will get people
thinking about habitat conservation. In *The Skeptical
Environmentalist*, Bjorn Lomborg puts a controversial argument that
not all dyed-in-the-wool Greens agree with...do you? Or *Fast Food
Nation* by Eric Schlosser...it'll be interesting to see how many of you
leave the room converted to vegetarian- or veganism, determined to
cut the cost of your meals to the earth and its inhabitants. Any one
of these, or perhaps E. F. Schumacher's *Small is Beautiful*, will
encourage readers to think hard about their lifestyles and their cost
to our environment in the short- and long-term. Even if each person
in a group of seven or eight makes only a small change – from

fitting an eco-friendly lightbulb to buying less meat, from composting their food waste to refusing to take their shopping home in a plastic bag – it helps a little. But imagine this replicated a hundred times, or a thousand... Taken up worldwide the positive impact on the environment would be tangible.

How do I do it?
Ask at your local library to see if they have any information on groups in your area. Phone a few friends and see if they would like to spend an evening a month getting together over a bottle of wine (or pot of tea) and talking about what they're reading. Go to your local library or you can get books on the high street or on the Internet.
Try www.ecobooks.co.uk; earthscan.co.uk or www.greenbooks.co.uk

Be well fed...

It's time to get out of the house. Amazing to think that environmentalism is so simple! This week we're sending you on a little trip – to a local farmers' market. There are over 380 in the country so most of you won't have far to go. www.farmersmarkets.net or your local council should be able to give you details of your nearest.

Farmers' markets were set up originally to give producers a better chance of getting a decent return for their products – be they animal, vegetable or mineral (water). Now farmers' markets are helping to beat global warming. Food accounts for between 1 and 3% of our individual CO_2 emissions. While choosing local food at a farmers' market is not going to save a huge amount of energy, compared to some of the measures in this book, it's a pleasurable experience that brings with it lots of social benefits. At Christmas time some of the markets have a festive feel with choirs, fairground attractions and a visit from Santa. Others post event updates on www.farmersmarkets.net, the website of The National Association of Farmers' Markets.

NAFM makes sure farmers stick to the rules. These state that farmers from a defined local area should be present, in person, to sell their own produce and that all products sold should have been grown, reared, caught, brewed, pickled, baked, smoked or processed by the stallholder.

Start a snowballing snowdome campaign!...

Time to get your unwanted souvenirs out for an armchair effort.
Water pollution comes in many forms, local and global, from
contaminant chemicals to thermal changes caused by carbon
emissions.

Stop Greenland turning green...

The US has failed to sign up to international protocols on climate
change. But there's only so much mail even the White House can
ignore – why not send them a snowdome to emphasise what's at
risk? Draft a letter including relevant facts and send it off with your
carefully packaged snowdome (and get your friends, family and
colleagues to do the same). Now is as good a time as any to start
making them sit up and take notice. If you don't, centuries of Inuit
culture will die out along with the indigenous people of Greenland
and other North Atlantic zones. The warming of the oceans is
melting the ice fields upon which the Inuit depend for their food
and clothing, putting the lives of hunters in danger as they cross
the thinning Permafrost. And not only that, but the currents of the

deep ocean bring with them record levels of chemical contaminants, which enter the food chain accumulating in the fatty tissues of the whales and seals that make up one-third of the Inuit diet. Average PCB and mercury levels are 20-50 times higher in the blood and breast milk of Greenland villagers than in urban areas of the USA and Europe*.

Where to send that snowdome...
President George W. Bush, The White House,
1600 Pennsylvania Avenue NW, Washington, DC 20500
If you don't have a snowdome handy, why not email a picture of a polar bear instead? Send it to: president@whitehouse.gov

*Arctic Monitoring and Assessment Programme, 2003

Get out and get fit...

Norman Tebbit will be long-remembered for his subtle hint to the unemployed: 'Get on your bike...' But it's not just the unemployed his dulcet toned phrase is relevant to. Do yourself a favour and try out your childhood friend anew: beg, borrow or buy a bike and sample the delights of the great outdoors before it's covered in concrete, or full of fumes.

What's in it for the landscape?

Global warming and climate change are a result of increases in greenhouse gas emissions: e.g. the carbon dioxide (CO_2) produced by burning fossil fuels (coal, oil, gas). The gases accumulate in the earth's atmosphere, trapping in heat. And one of the biggest contributions to this greenhouse effect is the CO_2 generated by the fossil fuel driven internal combustion engine, which powers almost every car journey. (Not only that, but the noxious cocktail of hydrocarbons, particulates, benzene, nitrogen oxides, aldehydes and trace metals that belch from the exhaust are also potent environmental toxins, inhaled by you, your family and friends and contaminating the food you eat.)

Cut your contribution to global warming and environmental pollution by choosing to cycle to work, to school, to the station. There are now over 8,000 miles of safe routes for cyclists thanks to an initiative known as the National Cycle Network.

So how do I find my local routes?
Check out www.sustrans.org.uk – you can download or print off maps, buy publications or take part in an event. If you're not on the net, give them a call: 0845 113 0065.

Make soil and save Earth...

Most of the rubbish you chuck in your wheelie bin can be recycled, but there's one big heap that can't: food scraps. Luckily, nature has provided us with the answer: composting. Your task this week is to start composting your food scraps, cardboard and waste paper products, such as kitchen towels.

You will need:
- A neat box with a lid (often called a kitchen caddy).
  These can be bought but any plastic container will do.
- A roll of compostable bin liners made from sweet corn (optional if you don't mind cleaning your kitchen caddy out every week – they're only sized to fit some bins).
- A compost bin, wormery (for small spaces) or a council pick up scheme.

And then just...
Fill the kitchen caddy with any kitchen scraps, cardboard boxes, loo rolls, paper tissues etc. until it's full. When it is full transfer the contents to the compost bin.

Here's a tip. Don't lay the cardboard flat in the kitchen caddy. The insects and microscopic organisms that turn the contents of your kitchen caddy into compost prefer cardboard scrunched into balls somewhere between the size of an egg and a small melon. It affords them nice living conditions with plenty of air.

What can't be put in the kitchen caddy?

Some things just don't compost. Non-biodegradable materials like metals, plastics, textiles and rubber are obvious examples; but also newspapers and magazines, which would be better off in the recycling bin. Some people feel funny about composting animal waste, bread, and cooked food at home, and the skins of citrus fruits can take a long time to compost, but lots of people have no problems composting all of these items. See CAT's *How to Make Soil and Save Earth* for more information (available from CAT Mail Order: tel. 01654 705959; www.cat.org.uk/shop).

Look for the invisible...

It's not always obvious what causes poor air quality. Years ago smoking was said to be good for the lungs. Fumes such as methane are invisible and deadly; others just irritating and unpleasant. Odours can set off asthma attacks. Common household materials can turn out to be deadly in themselves – such as asbestos; or the harbinger of unpleasant irritants – carpets. Dust itself can annoy or kill. This week's breathe easy challenge is to find out how you can improve the air quality inside your home. This may be as simple as finding out whether your house would benefit from an ioniser, or if there is a damp spot causing the growth of mould somewhere. Or it could be something bigger, such as replacing your carpets with a wooden floor. If you were looking for an excuse, you've got one.

Even if you don't act on all the information it's worth knowing what's going on in your home. For example, old paints often emit unpleasant gases but stripping away the paint from walls, ceilings and woodwork and replacing it with eco-paint is a job you'll need to plan. Normal practice is to use vinyl emulsion on walls and ceilings, and oil based gloss on internal and external woodwork, but concerns about the effects on human health of exposure to the volatile organic compounds in these paints mean they are gradually being replaced by water based vinyls. Natural or organic paints and stains use plant based solvents, fillers, and dyes – renewable resources which will biodegrade on disposal. All solvents are designed to evaporate – this is how paint dries. Although some people do have an allergic response to the solvents in natural paints, this is far less common and serious than is the case with petro-chemical solvents. www.alotoforganics.co.uk is an excellent starting point when looking for suppliers as it links to several other useful websites.

Save your company money by cutting waste...

Alan Knight works at B&Q. His job is to ensure the company is kept on the cutting edge of social, ethical and environmental issues. With a £60,000 salary attached to his job he is also expected to deliver cost savings and maximise commercial benefits from the company's enlightened policies. You may not be in a position to radically alter your company's consumption patterns but you could save your company money by introducing one or two small measures around the office. This is your task this week.

Start off by finding out more about the Environment Agency's Waste Minimisation Club (www.environment-agency.gov.uk/subjects/waste). In four years 120 clubs have shown 1000 members how to save £20 million by cutting waste. Then try www.envirowise.gov.uk; Envirowise say they save UK businesses up to £1000 per employee and, if your company employs fewer than 250 people, they will arrange a free Fast Track visit to your work place. Within one day an Envirowise advisor will identify opportunities for you to become more efficient with your resources and help plan to make these savings a reality.

Also try www.reducetheuse.co.uk for very small businesses, or www.wrap.org.uk and www.actionenergy.org.uk.

Company wastefulness comes in all shapes and sizes, so think laterally about where you can make the savings. Take your average vending machine, for example. Cups from vending machines get used once and cost your company to send to landfill. Save a Cup will take the cups and turn them into something useful: pens, pencils, rulers, key fobs, bins and so on. You can have any of them customised and use them to market your own company. (www.save-a-cup.co.uk).

Jump aboard a new hobby...

You're never too old to surf, but even if you can't see yourself in a Hawaiian shirt and shades your kids'll love it!

Join the SAS in their campaign to clean up our beaches...

That's Surfers Against Sewage, not the guys in fatigues... SAS aren't just tanned young men hanging out on boards, but an organisation devoted to making sure that the seas are fit to be enjoyed by all. Pollution from sewage outfall pipes is all too common around our coastlines. Over 300 million gallons of raw or partially treated sewage is discharged around the UK each day! That's along with the two million tonnes of toxic waste dumped into the sea every year. And it isn't just what you flush down the loo – there's the residue from rinsing paintbrushes in the sink, the bleach and chemicals in hair dyes from hundreds of hairdressers and the fats and oils from your washing up. Phew... So, even if you can't surf the seas, you can surf the shops and cut down on the c**p you pull the plug on by making the right consumer choices, or by pressing for industry, legislators and politicians to put an end to 'pump and dump' policies.

If you're too far inland to surf regularly check out the touring Longlife exhibition: with surfboards decorated by artists from Damien Hirst to Jamie Hewlett. Or send off for one of the education packs SAS produce to introduce the next generation to their campaigns through National Curriculum Citizenship work.

It's never too late...
- Surfers Against Sewage, Wheal Kitty Workshops, St Agnes, Cornwall, TR5 0RD. tel. 0845 4583001; www.sas.org.uk

Be kind to your kids...

It's difficult to combat 'pester power', but there are things you can do to ensure your kids get the best start in life.

What changes can I make that will actually do something to ensure there's a natural world left for them to enjoy?

Consumer power is huge: it drives the market in lots of retail areas (just ask Gerald Ratner or the men at M&S). You can make educated, environmental decisions about everything you buy.

- Clothing: try and make sure that nothing you put your children in contains PVC, in logos or elsewhere; where possible go for organic materials like cotton, wool or hemp in preference to synthetics. Try www.bao-bab.co.uk for eco- and child-friendly garments – they use natural colours that will encourage the planting of native dye plants)

- Skin care: avoid using products – soaps/shower gels/bubble bath, talcum, baby oil, skin creams etc. – containing foaming agents, parabens or aluminium. Check out your local health food shop or chemist for brands such as Weleda, or Green People (if hard to find locally try www.earthlets.co.uk). Avoid using products which may 'bio-accumulate' in children's bodies over a lifetime.

- Food: avoid processed foods wherever possible; buy and cook organic food and drink; keep the burgers and pizzas for special occasions – home-made is heaps better than fast food! Keep pesticides out of their diet and out of the fields.
- Toys: avoid PVC and other plastics that are liable to give off-gas from volatile organic chemicals; buy wooden toys or dolls made of cotton or wool, metal or inert plastics. If your local toy-barn can't help, the Internet is a valuable resource for research and mail order – just type 'natural toys' or 'wooden toys' into a search engine.

Be a plant lover...

Stop eating animal products. This has been a hard one to place in the year for reasons that I will explain in a moment. So far we have talked mostly about the global warming gas carbon dioxide but this is not the only global warming gas. In fact, methane is the more worrying greenhouse gas – it is twenty times more powerful than carbon dioxide. The only reason people don't talk about it as much is that we create much more carbon dioxide. However, whilst we can control CO_2 emissions by developing new technologies and making lifestyle choices, we can't stop animals burping and farting; and, believe it or not, farmed farts are now making a significant contribution to global warming. So much so, that the government of New Zealand has considered taxing its sheep farmers if they can't stop their sheep burping!

The reason this task has been difficult to place in the year is that whilst giving up animal products is probably one of the hardest things to do, and has relatively little impact compared to some of the other measures described in this book, it may become more important in the future: that is, once people and governments have done what they can to cut CO_2 emissions. If you were already thinking about going veggie, it's another good reason for doing so. Find out more about how animal farming affects the environment by visiting www.animalaid.org.uk

Rubbish incinerators...

Early one October morning in 2002 a group of Greenpeace volunteers invaded a waste incinerator in Sheffield, scaled its chimney and put it out of action for three days. This was part of an organised campaign to close down all 15 incinerators in Britain and prevent the building of another 150, planned as part of the government's waste strategy. Each year we produce 26 million tonnes of rubbish of which 2.5 million tonnes is burnt. This is roughly equivalent to the amount of rubbish we recycle.

Greenpeace thinks this is a shameful statistic when you consider the cocktail of poisonous chemicals an incinerator releases into the air. Visit www.greenpeace.org.uk, go to their incineration campaign page and click on the 'find out what operators don't tell you' link. Here you will find a cool interactive graphic which shows you just how stupid it is to burn mixed rubbish rather than sorting it for recycling.

The heat of the incinerator vaporises heavy metals such as lead and cadmium, and causes chemical reactions, which produce new toxic chemicals such as dioxins, PCBs and a variety of others. Although there are laws prohibiting excessive releases of these gases into the air they are regularly broken. The incinerator at Sheffield breached the limits 156 times in one year.

Your task this week is to support the incinerator campaign. The Greenpeace website has a map of sites and tells you if you have a Greenpeace Incinerator Buster team at work in your area. You can also get hold of a template to create a people's waste strategy for your area, leaflets and postcards to campaign and all the facts and figures you need to make a convincing case.

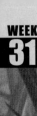

Create a wildlife haven at the bottom of the garden...

In exchange for a couple of days' work per year, sowing seed and mowing your patch of meadow, you can add to local biodiversity and perhaps help save a species or two from extinction.

Why is it needed?

In Britain, butterflies and some bird species have suffered declining populations due to both the destruction of their semi-natural habitats through changes in land management, and because areas of wholly natural habitat have become fewer and much farther apart. The abandonment of coppicing and marginal lowland grazing areas and increases in upland grazing, along with the grubbing out of hedgerows (between 1984 and 1990 76,000 miles of UK hedgerow was lost), means that many species are fewer in number. Since the 1940s 80% of chalk and limestone grassland has been lost, 75% of actively coppiced woodland and 40% of lowland heath. As a result numerous butterflies, including the High Brown Fritillary and Wood White, have suffered a 60-80% drop in numbers and five species, including the Large Copper and Large Blue, have become extinct. Even the common house sparrow is now considered threatened due to changes in building design – its nest sites are becoming harder to find with changes to roofs and eaves.

How do I attract wildlife into the garden?

- Send off for free booklet: The Birds in Your Garden from the RSPB (www.rspb.org.uk; tel. 01767 680551) and follow their advice, or check out their 'A-Z of wildlife in the garden' web pages
- Visit www.butterfly-conservation.org or phone 0870 7744309, they will be able to supply information on what to plant to attract butterflies into the garden (species such as buddleia, sedum and lavender)
- Adopt an area of urban wasteland and convert it into a community wildlife reserve

WEEK
31

Make sure you're getting a good deal from your council...

The Doorstep Recycling Act will soon require councils to collect at least two recyclates – the technical term for things that can be recycled – from your door. Some councils are already collecting seven different recylates in similar schemes. However, many campaigners feel the Act will lead to a huge range of inconsistencies across the country, with some communities enjoying a much better service from their councils than others. One trend is obvious even now – rural areas are doing much better than city areas. London boroughs Hackney and Tower Hamlets are bottom of the heap, along with Sunderland, Rochdale and Manchester, with recyling rates between 1 and 3%. The great urban areas, where most rubbish comes from, are being left behind.

Your task this week is to find out how well your council is doing and see how it intends to fulfill the requirements of the Doorstep Recycling Act. Look up your Waste Management Officer in the A-Z of council services in your phone book and make a quick call. If they are not able to tell you, ask them why and see if they can give you an answer within a couple of weeks. If you are not satisfied with the answer contact your council's Local Agenda 21 Officer, whose remit is to implement sustainable development at a local level. If the waste management team isn't addressing the recycling issue, the LA21 officer is the council insider to talk to. Then try your local councillor. A councillor can sit on the committee responsible for directing local authority policies on waste. If you don't get anywhere via these routes (and by this time you may well be a few weeks into your campaign) it might be time to join a local campaigning group like Friends of the Earth (www.foe.org.uk) and plan your next move (see week 37).

Adopt a local water course and invite your friends along to make its aquaintance...

Looking out for the natural environment doesn't have to be all hair shirts and sacrifices. You can have a laugh with your mates and get something positive done at the same time. You could even make it an alternative birthday bash and take a celebratory picnic along!

So how do I make it happen?

Thames21, a local agenda initiative, has an Adopt-A-River scheme for Old Father Thames that gets groups of interested volunteers together to work on regeneration schemes big and small. If you're local to the Thames give the organisers a ring and they'll sort you out with a team challenge for as few as ten people. At the end of their day of cleaning up the foreshore, staff from the Hilton, Rotherhithe, were rewarded by a visit from a female grey seal who checked out their achievements on the beach before swimming back out into the river! If you like the sound of it, but don't live within the M25, why not get in touch with Thames21 and ask for advice on how to set up a similar scheme for your local river or lake, even an urban canal? If the canal is your nearest waterway, there's a whole organisation dedicated to waterways restoration and they run Canal Camps you could take part in.

Useful contacts
· Thames21: tel. 020 7248 2916; www.thames21.org.uk
· Your local county or metropolitan council: look them up in the telephone book and ask to speak to the Local Agenda 21 officer
· The Waterway Recovery Group: tel. 01923 711114; www.wrg.org.uk

Help others to help themselves...

You can choose your level of difficulty for this one: you don't even have to leave the house if you want to do it the easy way. But maybe, if you get the chance and you're the adventure travel type, you could do it the hard way and travel to the source of the problem to make your point in person.

Got compassion fatigue – or can you imagine what it would be like to be in their shoes?

In December 2004, it will be twenty years since the Union Carbide factory in Bhopal, India, went into meltdown (a runaway exothermic reaction, for the scientists among you). A poison cloud of methyl isocyanate was released into the air over a 20km2 area – 8000 people were killed in the immediate aftermath and, thanks to persistent pollution in the local groundwater, the latest available figures (1994, since when measuring has ceased) record 120,000 people with exposure related symptoms. Dow Chemical, who bought the Bhopal disaster liability along with Union Carbide's business, have not yet committed to cleaning up the site of the abandoned factory. But there are opportunities for willing environmentalists to do something, to put a stop to the continuing abuse of the land and people in Bhopal, where Dow have failed.

So how do I get involved?

The armchair activist

- Take part in an email campaign to lobby Dow to clean up their mess
- Log on to www.greenpeace.org or www.bhopal.net

The hands-on volunteer

- Contact www.bhopal.org and join the Sambhavna Trust
- Travel to India and help out at Terry's Garden, an ayurvedic herbal medicine garden at the clinic treating survivors: collect rainwater – water that will be free of contamination – for irrigating crops

Dump the disposable diaper…

Bit more tricky this one – for a busy mum, at home or at work, the all-in-one, single use nappy has been a huge time saver, but – and it's a big but – it isn't a life-saver in environmental terms. However, there is a realistic alternative to pre-disposable drudgery.

What's in it for me and my baby?

For a start, you'll stop contributing your share to the 8 million disposable nappies thrown into British bins every single day of the year! Landfill pollution isn't the only problem, though…if your dirty disposable isn't being buried it's being burnt in an incinerator, releasing dioxins into the environment that then enter the food chain right down to mother's milk. Not a nice thought… Added to which, the cost to you the taxpayer of this mountain of toxic waste (the average disposable is a powerful chemical combo of super-absorbent synthetic granules, plastic and chlorine bleached paper pulp) is huge – Bristol City council spends £500,000 per year getting rid of it. Switching to real nappies will save you money at the tills too: you can buy sufficient real nappies and waterproofs for all your baby's nappy wearing days for the equivalent of 12 weeks' worth of disposables (costing approx. £70 according to the Women's Environmental Network Real Nappy campaign). But making the change doesn't mean going back to nappy buckets and Jeyes Fluid. There are now lots of local schemes for real nappy laundry services and cloth nappy suppliers, so you should be able to find a scheme to suit you and your lifestyle and protect your baby's future health at the same time.

So how do I do it?
A call to the Nappy Line should see you right: 01983 401959 – or visit www.wen.org.uk/nappies/nappies.htm for a full run-down on the diaper debate.

Be energy efficient...

By now, you've fitted low energy light bulbs, bought green electricity and have a fridge full of local food. For the next task you will need paper, pencil and a couple of free hours. If you get friends or family involved it'll make the job easier. This week's carbon challenge is to complete a full energy audit on your home. As you know, 25% of all our CO_2 emissions come from energy created to be used in the home. Although buying green electricity is a good option it is always better to save energy than use it. Also, by far the biggest energy demands in the average home are space and water heating, and cooking – and in most cases these particular energy needs will not be met by electricity.

Start your energy audit by working out how much energy you need to make your home function. Go round the house and make a list of all the energy demands your home makes, including all electrical appliances, heating and cooking systems. Now try and work out how many hours a week you use each appliance. After you've got all this information together you need to find out how much energy each appliance needs to make it work. With some appliances it may be obvious because it says what it requires on the packet – i.e. a 3kW electric heater uses 3kW of electricity every hour it is on. Others may have it in small print on the appliance or in the instructions. If it's not easy to find you can get estimates of average power consumption for standard appliances from your local Energy Advice Centre. Once you have identified your energy use you'll need some good advice on how to cut it. Get this free from an Energy Advice Office, or buy a copy of CAT's *The Energy Saving House*.

Work with community campaign groups...

Week 32's challenge was to find out how your council plans to meet the requirements of the Doorstep Recycling Act. The Act will require councils to collect at least two recyclates from your doorstep. If you live in the right area your council will collect seven; in the wrong area only the mandatory two. This seems a bit unfair since keen recyclers will have to lug the rest of their rubbish to the nearest supermarket car park or recycling centre. As week 48's challenge is to ditch your car (oh yes – we said it got harder) this is going to take some thinking about. Actually we do offer some good alternatives to car ownership, before you close the book completely.

If you don't like this state of affairs, or think it penalises people who can't afford or are unable to drive (for example, because of disability), think about how you could turn your local authority from a C- to an A grade recycler. Everyone can do better, given the right encouragement. This week's challenge is to join or set up a campaigning group that will help you to get the recycling services you want in your area. As the Act will not require councils to introduce even the basic collection service for several years, now is the time to get them thinking about the issue. Friends of the Earth has 200 local community groups across the country and produces a pack of six free publications showing you how to campaign in your local area. It also provides media training sessions for community campaigners covering photography and press release writing. Visit www.foe.org.uk

Rewire your house and make it safe twice over...

Most of us in the UK live in houses with wiring systems over 20 years old – how long is it since you had yours checked? If it needs an overhaul you'll be presented with an opportunity to do your bit towards ridding the earth of one of its most common toxic contaminants.

So why worry about my wires?

It's all down to the plastic sheathing. Chances are that all your electrics will be covered in PVC – or polyvinyl chloride, to give it its full name. PVC is the second most commonly used plastic in the world and the most harmful to the environment. It is made using industrial chlorine. All of the other products made with this chemical have been banned or phased out and yet PVC lives on – despite the fact that in most cases less problematic substances, from glass, metal, paper and ceramics to chlorine free plastics, can be used in its place. The problem is most acute in terms of the waste created during manufacture and on disposal: not only are dioxins and hydrochloric acid (a contributor to acid rain) produced during manufacture, but also on incineration. Added to which, PVC isn't ideal for a lot of applications and requires equally toxic additives such as pthalates (to supply plasticity), fungicides and heavy metals for colour, all of which add to the dangers involved in disposal. One Canadian warehouse fire released levels of dioxin 66 times higher than permitted, accounting for a 4% increase in Canada's 1997 emissions total*. Frankly, we can do without PVC and, for the sake of the food chain, we should.

Where can I get the alternatives?
- Telephone the CAT free information line for suppliers:
  0845 330 8373; 01654 705989

*Greenpeace International, www.greenpeace.org

Say goodbye to cheese-on-toast and cappucino...

Not an easy one for the glutton, but a personal sacrifice that could help put a stop to the UK's biggest water pollutant. Believe it or not, giving up on dairy foods will do just that.

Cut water pollution at the same time as cutting your cholesterol!

The agriculture sector was responsible for 150 water pollution incidents in 2002, and of those the dairy industry was the source of more than twice as many as any other sector*. Sewage in run-off from dairy farms is high in nitrates, which find their way into rivers and groundwater. The big problems are caused by nutrients such as nitrates getting into water in concentrations that adversely affect the ecology of rivers and lakes, increasing the production of algae and plants beyond natural levels. Communities of algae can reduce water clarity, diminishing native aquatic plant growth; they can also impact on the oxygen levels leading to invertebrate and fish deaths. By the middle of 2002, 86 rivers, 16 lakes/reservoirs and 10 estuaries in the UK had been identified as Sensitive Areas** to be monitored for their levels of nutrient damage. The upside is that things are getting better: in 2002 29% of rivers had high concentrations of nitrate as opposed to 32% in 2000, so cutting out your contribution will help keep this downward trend.

So what's the alternative if I can't face tea without milk?

- There are a number of non-dairy products such as rice, soya or other grain based alternatives to be found in health food shops and supermarkets: from rice milk to soya yogurts, olive oil spreads to vegan ice-cream
- The Vegan Society will be happy to help if you're having trouble: www.vegansociety.com; tel. 01424 427393

---

*   Environment Agency:
    Agricultural pollution incidents by source in England and Wales, 2002

** Environment Agency website: eutrophication (www.environment-agency.gov.uk)

Become a school governor...

This is going to eat into some of your precious free time, but giving up a bit of time now could ensure the earth has a future.

Why should I?

Lead by example and encourage good habits from an early age... It is far more likely that the world will change with a lot of people making small changes rather than just a few giving up all the advances of the 20th century! If you can persuade a school full of children – the next generation of workers – to each live a little more sustainably, then think of the changes they might encourage in others as they reach adulthood, through word of mouth, through their purchasing power, through their political choices. Once you are a governor, there's a lot you can do: encourage parents not to drive their kids to school – start a 'Walking-Bus' scheme instead (www.walkingbus.com); older children can get on their bikes (put in hand RoSPA National Cycling Proficiency Scheme training); set aside some outside space for a wildlife garden (encouraging organic growing and wildlife conservation); put recycling bins for rubbish and a compost bin for food scraps, cardboard and garden waste in the playground; talk to the education authority about sourcing their energy from renewable resources, buying recycled paper products and building new facilities from environmental materials. No doubt you can think of other positive changes, too.

So, how do I become a school governor?

- Contact your local school to ask if they need a new governor – if not, the local education authority (in the phone book) will be able to help you find a school or advise on opportunities
- The School Governors' One-Stop Shop recruits governors for inner city schools and areas with many vacancies: 64 Essex Road, London N1 8LR; tel: 0870 241 3883; www.sgoss.org.uk

Find your inner sailor...

Now you're getting into week 41 it's time to up the ante. Your home is running on renewable energy. You can't remember the last time you changed a light bulb and thanks to an energy audit your energy bills are lower than they've ever been before. Your carbon challenge this week is to see if you can ditch your next air flight in favour of a greener alternative. This is when the regular business flyers in the audience start to head for the door – but even if you don't actually take the alternative you should at least know what the alternatives are (if they exist at all), what they cost, and how inconvenient or convenient it is to take them. Even if you have to cross oceans and continents there are alternatives – from the more exotic and quite often less expensive options such as hitching a ride with a cargo ship to the US (www.strandtravel.co.uk) and crewing a sailing boat to the Bahamas (small ad's in sailing magazines), to the more obvious trains and buses. If your next trip is a holiday, think about taking a green holiday in Britain as a volunteer (www.nationaltrust.org.uk) or, at the other end of the luxury scale, taking the Orient Express to one of several destinations (www.world-rail-tickets.net).

The truth about air travel is that it just doesn't add up for the environment. A passenger making a long haul flight from London to the USA generates as much carbon dioxide as the average British car driver does in a year. If you can't avoid flights then you could lobby governments to put money into generating cleaner alternatives. At the moment the UK Government subsidises air flight to the tune of £7 billion through tax breaks; there is no excise duty on aviation fuel, and no VAT on fuel or passenger tickets. Air travel costs the average UK taxpayer £500 a year and gives the industry an unfair competitive advantage over bus and rail.

Quit the hit...

As we're near the end it's time for something really tough. Give up smoking. Or if you don't smoke, persuade someone else to give up. And if neither you, your friends, your close family, distant relatives nor in-laws smoke, then take everyone out to a smoke free pub (www.ash.org.uk for a list) and support smoke-free environments. There are only about 30 at the moment (out of a possible 60,000) but industry bosses will create more if they are commercially viable. The Laurel Pub Company is setting an example by turning 50 of its 635 pubs into smoke-free zones. Giving up smoking is going to take more than a week, but if you need some extra reasons – apart from the obvious ones such as the increased risk of lung cancer, heart disease, cot deaths and so on – then find out more about why tobacco is one of the most destructive crops on the planet (www.ash.org.uk again).

To get you started here are some of the facts about tobacco production:

- An estimated 5.5 million pounds of methyl bromide (an ozone-depleting chemical) is used by the tobacco industry on its crops
- 200,000 hectares of woodland destroyed each year for tobacco
- It takes 12 cubic metres of wood to cure every tonne of tobacco In one region of Malawi, nearly 80% of the wood cut down is used for tobacco production, even though tobacco farmers make up only 3% of the farmers in the area
- 10 to 20 million people could be fed by food crops grown instead of tobacco
- Tobacco growers are susceptible to an occupational illness known as green tobacco sickness

Try www.giveupsmoking.co.uk

Run for more than fun...

It'll take you time to train for this, but not the millions of years it has taken for the Pacific Ocean to become the incredibly rich and diverse marine habitat it is now...

Start by walking, end by changing your world...

The Ocean Conservancy in the US is the beneficiary of the Pacific Shoreline marathon, which covers a route adjacent to the glorious scenery of the Californian coast. The money raised for every mile covered supports the Conservancy's mission to protect ocean ecosystems and the diversity of marine wildlife (threatened by the change in thermal currents such as the Gulf Stream). But you don't have to fly half way round the world to do your bit. The majority of runners traversing London each April do so in aid of the charity of their choice – why not do it for the oceans? The Ocean Conservancy's UK equivalent is the Marine Conservation Society – their current projects include work on the protecton of coral reefs, marine turtle conservation and education programmes for sustainable tourism.

Put your best foot forward by contacting:

- www.mcsuk.org
- www.oceanconservancy.org
- www.london-marathon.co.uk – follow links to 'charity places' or contact your chosen charity direct and ask if they have a scheme for sponsored marathon entries (telephone numbers in Yellow Pages under Charitable and Voluntary Organisations).

Lump the pump...

Umm... this one's going to sound quite similar to week 48, but there's no getting away from it. If you really want to improve air quality you're going to have to do something about that car. We may not be stupefying our children with lead any more but the UK's National Air Quality Information Archive still rates petrol as the number one air pollutant. No wonder when you consider that petrol pump pollutants include carbon monoxide, oxides of nitrogen (NOx), volatile organic compounds (VOCs) and particulates. And photochemical reactions resulting from the action of sunlight on nitrogen oxide and VOCs leads to the formation of ozone (good up where there's a hole in the sky, bad at ground level). And NOx influences acid rain.

Read week 48 for a good range of options (electric cars, mopeds, bicycles etc) and, if that isn't enough, try moving to a place that encourages the alternatives by putting cars second. Car free zones in cities are becoming increasingly popular but the best housing development in Britain is the BedZED, or Beddington Zero Emission

Development (www.bedzed.org.uk). BedZED is the first housing development to have a legally binding green transport plan as a condition of planning permission. They plan to cut car use amongst their residents by 50% over the next ten years by providing residential office spaces, on-site facilities such as a healthy living centre with childcare facilities, and Internet shopping links with a local supermarket for bulk buying. There is less noise, less on-site pollution and a safer environment for children. There is also generous bike storage, on-site charging for electric cars and plans for a car pool. www.bedzed.org.uk

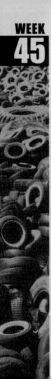

Start your own business...

Way back at week 5 we introduced you to David Owen and his metal sculptures. If you've followed from week one to here you will know by now that, with the support of both the government and consumers, recycled products are going to be big business. If you spent a while looking through the websites of Rethink Rubbish and the Waste Resources Action Programme (WRAP) you will have come across some of the success stories. If you've developed a real taste for recycling it may be time to look into starting your own business. The last rubbish challenge is to come up with an idea for a new recycled product, run it up a flagpole and see if it flies.

Start off by getting some inspiration from other people. Look back at the products you have come across; find out as much as you can about the companies that produce them; how and when they were set up and how well they have done. Get to know the recycled materials suppliers and find out what rubbish is available for processing. If you haven't already done so look at www.wrap.org.uk. WRAP runs a Business Development Service, which marries funders to producers and can provide free advice about the recycling sector. It mainly concentrates on glass, plastics, wood, paper, aggregates and organics. If you're serious about the idea read its market research papers. For general and local business advice go and talk to your local Business Link officer (www.businesslink.org). Not only will they be able to give you information about the local business environment they will also help you get to grips with the mechanics of starting your own business.

Build your own green dream home...

This one's a biggie! Not all of us are able to up sticks and self-build, but the same basic rules apply to ordinary DIY...

What do I do and why?

First choose your site: most eco-friendly of all is a 'brownfield' site, i.e. a patch of land that has been built on before. Or, renovate an existing building – but make sure you register a change of use if it was not previously residential. Next choose your architect/builder: the Association for Environment Conscious Building has a directory of members. Finally, make sure that your design takes into account every aspect of green building, from materials to design for energy efficiency and conservation, water conservation and quality, sewage treatment and energy supply. What you build with impacts on the local and global habitat. Choose lime over cement and you will cut your contribution to air pollution. Choose fsc timber over plywood from tropical hardwoods and you'll help stop illegal logging. Choose a wood pellet boiler over storage heaters and you'll help cut down on the need for nuclear electricity and its associated waste problem.

But seriously...

Making positive changes to existing housing stock really is the best place to start. It is better to reduce the need for new housing, reuse old housing stock, or recycle its elements, than to build anew from scarce resources. Making improvements to the energy efficiency of your current home, conserving water, and making sure that when something needs to be replaced it is replaced with eco-friendly materials and products is perhaps more important than making one momentous change...

Useful contacts

- AECB: Association for Environment Conscious Building, PO Box 32, LLandysul, SA44 5ZA; www.aecb.net
- www.cat.org.uk or www.ecobooks.co.uk: CAT's publication *The Whole House Book* is the green builder's bible!

WEEK
46

If you can't beat them, join them...

Devoting your working life to environmental politics is quite a
challenge, but if you really want to have a voice at policy level then
becoming a candidate for anything from your local council to
central government or the European Union is the route to national
and international changes for the better.

So how do I do that?
First things first, find out which political party holds views closest
to your own and then join up: they'll explain what's involved and
how to go about it. If you wish, you can stand as an independent.
Contact the Elections and Electoral Services Officer for information
and a guide on the nomination and election process for local and
district councils. To be eligible you must be 21 or over on the day
nominations close and be a British, Commonwealth or Irish
Republic citizen (or of another state within the European Union) and
included on the electoral register for the council's area. If you can
satisfy the first two of the above conditions but not the third, you
must have either lived or owned property or worked within the

district for the 12 months immediately before the election day. Unlike parliamentary candidates, you won't have to pay a deposit before standing for election, but you will have to complete a nomination paper and submit it before the statutory deadline. Each nomination paper must be verified by ten signatories, a proposer, a seconder and eight others included on the electoral register from the ward you wish to represent. Once elected you are on your way...look out for opportunities on the Planning Committee – a good place to start making positive changes.

Useful contacts:
Look up your local council offices, or the political party of your choice on www.google.co.uk or www.askjeeves.co.uk

Be (car) free...

The last week of the carbon challenge and, short of giving up modern life altogether to live in a cave, the biggest thing you can do for the environment now is to trade in your car for a bike, a good pair of walking shoes or a season ticket... Or, if you really can't do this, buy a car that uses less fuel, or even better, one of the growing range of eco-friendly fuels now on the market. Just as with the light bulb, the principles of car mechanics have hardly changed in the last hundred years. Pistons go up and down, wheels go around, motion is created, and out of the back comes a whole lot of pollution. Whilst innovations in motor engine design and the study of aerodynamics have improved fuel efficiency, these improvements have hardly kept pace with increases in the frequency and length of car journeys. Switch to Liquid Petroleum Gas (www.energyshift.co.uk), electric or an electric/petrol/hybrid combination (www.eva.co.uk or www.zeropollution.com).

Most of us use cars inefficiently. Not only do we leave seats empty when we travel, we let our expensive piece of machinery sit idle for most of its working life. Any business with such an attitude would soon go bust. www.carclubs.org.uk have come up with a clever alternative: this is an organised car share scheme and operates around the country. Members use cars kept within ten minutes walk of their home and can borrow them any time of day for anything from one hour upwards. Anna Semlyen has lots of useful information and practical advice for anyone wanting to give up their car in her book *Cutting Your Car Use* (order from CAT). Visit her website – www.cuttingyourcaruse.co.uk

Become a solar guerilla!...

Not the easiest of weeks, this... You'll need a certain amount of gumption, quite a lot of cash for the kit, some electrical engineering skill and a willingness to break the law in the name of renewable energy.

Is it worth the risk?

It's certainly worth it for the planet, in respect of the polluting fossil fuel energy it makes redundant. The movement originates in the USA where homeowners are installing photovoltaic arrays and generating solar electricity that they then feed back into the grid. When your electricity output outstrips your energy demand the electricity from your panels goes out into the grid – and your meter runs backwards! The legal problem is that you aren't supposed to feed electricity into the grid, at least not without permission and an awful lot of bureaucracy! What you must ensure is that your system is safe – for you and for the electricity worker, who may be working on power lines receiving current from your system when the grid is down. The beauty is that there are now, in the States at least, inverters that will switch themselves off when the grid goes down, ensuring the safety of the workers in hard hats. Given that we don't get that much reliable sunshine in the UK, you might want to become a wind or hydro power guerilla instead. The principle is the same: you need the kit and an inverter for your grid connection.

But seriously...
You don't need to do it on this basis, it is quite possible – and CAT would recommend it over becoming an urban guerilla! – for you to produce your own electricity and sell any surplus back to the grid. Telephone the CAT Information Department on 0845 330 8373 or 01654 705989 and ask how it's done. For some background see www.homepower.com

Tax yourself...

Most of the goods we buy do not reflect their true environmental cost. When we buy a product we pay for labour, materials, transportation and so on but we do not pay for the cost of ill-health due to pollution, flood damage resulting from global warming, coastal erosion, deforestation, loss of species and so on. In fact we are discouraged from buying environmental products because they are invariably the more expensive alternative. This week's task is to change your buying habits by creating your own environmental tax.

The idea is simple. Each time you buy something that isn't eco, put a percentage of the cost to one side. It doesn't have to be real money. It could be just a paper sum. Set the tax at whatever level you like, whatever you think is appropriate. You could look at a range of comparable prices for environmentally responsible goods and work out the difference. For example: organic-v-non organic. Find out more about the idea of New Economics, the study of socially and environmentally responsible economic policy, by visiting the website of The New Economics Foundation (www.neweconomics.org).

If you are setting the money aside for real then you should do something special with it, be it saving it for an eco-holiday, putting it towards the cost of energy efficiency improvements or donating it to an environmental charity. Invest the money in an ethical bank or building society. Buy some more books. Take a course. Treat yourself to a massage. Use the knowledge in this book to reinvest in yourself, your community and your planet. Good luck!

Want to save the planet? Make it your job...

There is a lot we can do in our spare time to make the world a better place, but you can also help make changes in the eight hours you are at work. And you don't have to be an environment specialist to do it.

How do I do it?

You can start small by making an effort to persuade your current bosses to do an environmental audit of the company's activities – make sure you reduce office/factory consumption of materials and waste output, recycle what you can and reuse everything possible. But what about making a big change? It's always easier to change something from the inside. How about getting a job in an industry not known for its environmental stance? Why not work for change from within? Join an aggregates group and work with the Environment Agency towards making their activities as eco-friendly as possible; join an electricity company and help progress the change to renewable energy sources, e.g. from oil to solar; if your background is in retail join a supermarket chain and lobby for the increased stocking of organic produce and the composting of food waste on-site at store level – after all, it'll generate a saleable product! If your company doesn't have an Environment Officer or Environmental Policy, suggest they create a policy and a position (which, of course, you could then apply for). It doesn't matter what your area of skill, experience or interest, you will be able to find something that you can change for the better.

Useful contacts

- www.environment-agency.gov.uk (for lists of annual good/bad performers and pollution incidents)
- www.environmentjob.co.uk (for listings of jobs in the environment sector)
- www.ecobooks.co.uk (to purchase a copy of *The Sustainable Careers Handbook*)

Become President of the United States...

The UK's Chief Scientific Officer Sir David King has described current US policy on global warming as a bigger threat to world security than terrorism. He attacked the Bush Presidency for not doing enough to reduce America's contribution to global carbon dioxide emissions, which now stands at 20% – higher than any other country in the world. Americans produce more carbon emissions per person than any other nationality on the planet and, since they refused to sign up for the Kyoto agreement on global warming, this looks unlikely to change.

The biggest thing you could do for the world is become President of the United States, sign up immediately to the Kyoto agreement, commit every US citizen to reducing their carbon emissions to a proportionately fair amount and lead the world to a more prosperous and peaceful future. Bit of a tough week this one. For one thing, if you're not a natural born American citizen you will never become president, which seems a bit unfair considering the impact America is having on your life. (Even the new, Austrian born Governor of California, Arnold Schwarzenegger, will never make it.)

Hasta la vista Mr President....
And then there's the small question of the $100 million you'll need to get from corporate interests to stand for president. Which brings us to Mr Bush's problem – oil: a bigger threat to global security than terrorism. Friends of the Earth recently calculated that ExxonMobil (Esso to you and me) and its predecessors caused 4.7% to 5.3% of the world's man-made carbon dioxide emissions between 1882 and 2002. And where did Bush get most of his money from to become president? ExxonMobil.

But if you can't join 'em', beat 'em': 11 American multinationals have experienced falling or stagnant 'brand power' thanks to Bush. Visit www.saveourearth.co.uk to find out more.

That's it, the big one, do this and the world will be fit for the future!

As well as being Britain's leading supplier of practical green publications, The Centre for Alternative Technology is also...

- Europe's leading green tourist attraction
- A membership organisation: tel. 01654 705988 to join or email members@cat.org.uk
- Britain's biggest mail order supplier of green books and products: tel. 01654 705959 for a catalogue or email mailorder@cat.org.uk
- An educational charity offering 40 weekend leisure and professional development courses (01654 705981; courses@cat.org.uk), day visits to schools (01654 705983; ann.mcgarry@cat.org.uk) and residential group visits (01654 705982; cabins@cat.org.uk)
- A positive forward thinking organisation to support (tel. 01654 705976 or email fundraising@cat.org.uk if you would like to make a donation towards our work)

Or visit one of our websites to find out more: www.cat.org.uk; www.ecobooks.co.uk